ON INTERIOR DESIGN

FOR MY SEVEN "BOYS"—THE BEST PART OF ME.

PENNY DRUE BAIRD **ON INTERIOR DESIGN**

Foreword by Jamie Drake

images
Publishing

Published in Australia in 2018 by
The Images Publishing Group Pty Ltd
ABN 89 059 734 431

Offices

Australia
6 Bastow Place
Mulgrave, Victoria 3170
Australia
Tel: +61 3 9561 5544

United States
6 West 18th Street 4B
New York, NY 10011
United States
Tel: +1 212 645 1111

books@imagespublishing.com
www.imagespublishing.com

The Images Publishing Group Reference Number: 1469

NATIONAL LIBRARY OF AUSTRALIA

A catalogue record for this book is available from the National Library of Australia

Title: On Interior Design: Penny Drue Baird // Penny Drue Baird
ISBN: 9781864707847

This title was commissioned in IMAGES' New York office and produced as follows:
Editorial Gina Tsarouhas, *Graphic design | Production* Nicole Boehringer *Thanks to* Rebecca Gross (copyediting)

PHOTO CREDITS
© Brittany Ambridge 11
© Antoine Bootz 12–13, 16–17, 18–19, 21, 22, 23, 24–25, 32, 33, 34–35, 36, 37, 38, 54, 55, 62, 63, 64, 65, 66–67, 68, 69, 70–71, 72, 73, 80, 84–85, 92–93, 96, 102–3, 110–11, 134–35, 136, 137, 138, 139, 140–41, 142–43, 148–49, 152, 153, 156–57, 166–67, 174, 177, 182–83, 186, 187, 190–91, 192–93, 196, 197, 198, 199, 200, 201, 203 right, 204–5, 210–11, 216–17, 220, 224–25, 227, 228–29, 232, 234–35, 236–37, 240–41, 245, 254, 255
© Maya Citron *back cover*
© Francis Hammond 20, 28–29, 30, 31, 39, 44–45, 46 left, 47 right, 48, 49, 50–51, 52–53, 74–75, 88, 89, 90–91, 100, 112–13, 118–19, 120, 121, 122, 123, 124–25, 128–29, 132–33, 147, 150–51, 154–55, 158, 159, 162–63, 168, 169, 170, 172–73, 176, 188–89, 218–19, 226, 233, 238, 239, 252–53, 260, 261, 262, 263, 264, 266–67, 268–69
© Ira Montgomery 42–43, 76–77, 78–79, 97, 98–99, 146, 184, 185, 205, 214–15, 244, 246, 247, 248, 249, 250–51, 258–59
© David Papazian 40–41, 82–83, 108–109, 126–27, 160, 161, 206, 207, 221, 222, 223, 265
© Durston Saylor *front cover*, 26–27, 60–61, 114–15, 116–17, 212, 213, 243
© Nick Sargent 46 right, 47 left, 56–57, 86, 87, 100–101, 104–105, 106, 107, 144, 145, 175, 178–79, 180–81, 202, 203 left, 208, 209, 256, 257

Printed on GoldEast matte art paper by Everbest Printing Investment Limited, in Hong Kong/China

CONTENTS

“THE ESSENCE OF INTERIOR DESIGN WILL ALWAYS BE ABOUT PEOPLE AND HOW THEY LIVE. IT IS ABOUT THE REALITIES OF WHAT MAKES FOR AN ATTRACTIVE, CIVILIZED, MEANINGFUL ENVIRONMENT, NOT ABOUT FASHION OR WHAT'S IN OR WHAT'S OUT. THIS IS NOT AN EASY JOB.”

—Albert Hadley

FOREWORD

Jamie Drake

The world of interior design is both magical and mysterious. Creating fantastic rooms takes guts and instinct, but also skill and understanding. Penny Drue Baird's interiors show a true master at work. For decades, Baird has fashioned sets for living, both for herself and for her lucky legion of loyal clients. Her portfolio of projects extends throughout the United States and stretches across the ocean to Europe. Published extensively in the most prominent design publications and honored as a member of the AD100, Penny's talents are widely recognized.

The artist inside Penny Drue Baird draws for inspiration on her beloved second home, France. Her first visit to Paris took place in her senior year of high school, and she fell in love immediately: it was, as the French say, a coup de foudre, a stroke of lightning. A new world sprang to vivid three-dimensional life: enchantment, enlightenment, refinement, and detail. On her plate were the riches of Escoffier and Le Vau. Béarnaise and bordelaise were connected to plaster *patisserie*, passementerie, and brocatelle effortlessly in the ingénue's mind. The exquisite architectural detail of the seventeenth and eighteenth centuries, the limestone piles of the Haussmannian nineteenth century, and the soignée Art Deco of the twentieth century imprinted themselves into her eyes and have resulted in decades of sophisticated work.

Establishing her firm Dessins in 1985, Penny embarked on a career that has allowed her to explore a great stylistic diversity: grand homes, coastal retreats, and mountain lodges have all sprung to vivacious reality. Her love of travel has provided endless springs of inspiration and discovery. Walking the avenues and streets of New York and Paris (Madison Avenue, Bond Street, and Orchard Street; the rues Cambon and Saint Honoré, avenue Montaigne), her eyes absorb both big picture and minute detail, not to mention the subtleties in between.

In Penny's fourth book, *On Interior Design*, she explains in detail the alchemy she employs so effortlessly. What fabric goes on what sofa next to which chair on what rug? What lamp, with which lampshade, belongs on what table? These are not random and isolated decisions; indeed, the more consciously they are made the more successful they are. It is these decisions that Penny explains to us, sharing the magic she uses to create ravishing rooms, spaces that are smart and chic and oh so pleasing.

Enjoy!

"OBJECTS CREATED IN VERY DIFFERENT TIMES AND BY ARTISTS OF VERY DIFFERENT CULTURES CAN STILL GO WELL TOGETHER AND EVEN COMPLEMENT ONE ANOTHER SO LONG AS THEY POSSESS ONE IMPORTANT ELEMENT IN COMMON—QUALITY."

—David Rockefeller

INTRODUCTION

I have been interested in interior design for as long as I can remember. While comfortably designed kitchens, living rooms, and bedrooms are integral to many homes and family life, daily conversation about the interior design process is not. Yet in my home it was.

We frequently discussed the aesthetics of home décor—ideas, creative process, and outcomes—and so it is hardly surprising that I grew up to embrace design as my life's work. I was so aware of and interested in design, as one is attracted to art or cuisine, that it evolved from a hobby to a career. As an undergrad at the University of Rochester, I painted the moldings of my college friends' dorm rooms; as a graduate student in Chicago, I upholstered walls with sheets and glued shells onto the bathroom mirror of my rental apartment. I look back on twentieth-century design with a knowing eye because I lived it. Design shifted back and forth between traditional and modern and it continues to influence the world we live in today.

I am often asked to lecture on the tidal wave of changes in design during the twentieth century; many were radical, and I see that trend continuing. Whether you are starting out at 25, coming into your own at 35, or refreshing your environment at 65, the warp speed of technological change has vastly increased the audience and their ability to acquire furnishings, lighting, materials, artworks, and objects.

Looking back, design development followed a linear trajectory for hundreds of years. Furnishings and necessities slowly evolved, improved, and became more embellished and many of the variations between design periods were a function of taste, and taste alone. Colors, patterns, and materials influenced the shape and decoration of heavy or light, opulent or austere, and intricately or simply designed pieces, but their basic underlying form remained the same.

Much of the furniture produced before the 1920s is labeled "traditional" by today's standards. But design became more innovative from the 1920s onward as the necessities of daily life and the psychology and realities of daily living changed. While there have been tumultuous political and social changes throughout history, they did not always result in dramatic changes in design.

I view World War I as the pivotal moment at which interior design changed forever. During the women's suffrage movement and the war, women went to work at what were considered "men's jobs." Empowered suddenly, and for the first time, women changed their attire, throwing off their corsets and wearing loose clothing (think the fashionable young women, or flappers, of the 1920s). In similar fashion, people wanted simple, clean-line furnishings at home rather than the heavy damasks, velvets, and monumental furniture of previous generations. Stylish rooms created by designers of their day still look entirely what we call "modern" today. Design as a reaction to psycho-social stimuli was palpable.

We then saw an ongoing switch between traditional and modern design throughout the twentieth century. As recently as the 1990s, traditional was back in its full nineteenth-century glory. Modern life was conducted in surroundings of uber-traditional décor, in distinct contrast to the brash and bold postmodern design of the previous decade.

Then, as we turned the corner of the twenty-first century, people felt encumbered by the traditional—the chintz, the "brown furniture" (English-style furnishings), and the Louis and their accoutrements, as well as the formality that surrounded these looks. They were replaced by a forward-looking approach and the desire to shed the old and begin anew. With the new century also came the internet, giving people access to more design—more everything—than ever before.

A new look emerged with the new era, but we had seen elements of it before. Pale, neutral color schemes reigned and everything suddenly became gray or white. Was this new? Well, we had gray and white in the 1970s. Tables were made with fine and exotic materials such as parchment (1970s again) and shagreen (1920s). Furniture forms shifted from traditional to contemporary with clean and simple lines. Was this new? We had seen many of these forms before as well. A simultaneous revival of mid-century design continues today.

The look that emerged in the twenty-first century has been called "transitional." This moniker has no meaning however—a period is transitional if it is a shift from one thing to another, and this is an assessment that can be made only in retrospect. More on point, the look can be described as anything from updated traditional to contemporary casual.

What is happening in design in the new millennium reflects, as is commonly the case, a rejection of what came before and a search for a new voice. Whatever our age or stage, we strive for a fresher outlook, an easier way to live, and our own space in which to do it.

While the world of interior design constantly evolves, trends are easily spotted as designers' and architects' works are published in print and online. But I believe trends should be avoided. Good design is always the result of a selective eye, and creativity and a personal touch are more meaningful in home décor than any adherence to design trends. Ideas and inspiration can be derived from travel, history, art, culture, fashion, and daily life, and they merge in rich layers of color, texture, pattern, art, accessories, and personality.

It is an exciting time to be interior designing. There is an enormous array of merchandise to peruse and then pursue, and homeowners can create a look that expresses their own personality and values. Indeed, individuality is the essence of interior design today. Don't be coerced by what surrounds you; instead, create an environment in which your needs are met with your personal style flourishes.

ARCHITECTURE
ART AND
DETAIL

“I DON’T THINK THAT ARCHITECTURE IS ONLY ABOUT SHELTER, IS ONLY ABOUT A VERY SIMPLE ENCLOSURE. IT SHOULD BE ABLE TO EXCITE YOU, TO CALM YOU, TO MAKE YOU THINK.”

—Zaha Hadid

I have always believed that fabulous architecture trumps fabulous design. An elaborate castle with simple furniture is more compelling than an intricately decorated, yet sterile white box. Unfortunately, castles are few and far between, but there is a renaissance of diverse architectural styles and forms, which are providing homeowners with striking features and details.

If your home doesn't fall into the category of fabulous architecture, then consider adding architectural details. Moldings, crowns, coves, baseboards, paneling, beams, wainscoting, beadboards, and columns can be incorporated in varied combinations to create a contemporary, traditional, or eclectic look and feel. This is where travel and art history can play a role. Moldings can also be applied creatively with tape or paint. Run beadboard, a simple and easily available type of paneling, in two directions—horizontally below a chair rail and vertically from chair rail to crown.

EARTH FROM ABOVE

Architectural definition does not have to rely solely on the structure of a building. Lighting, color, and furnishings can be used to define or highlight the architectural detail of a room. It is a question of style, placement, balance, and creativity. Style and placement of furniture can help create architectural punctuation, and the positioning of furniture establishes architectural lines. A pair of tall bookcases on either side of a sofa balance a fireplace or doorway on the opposite side of a room. A particular style of furniture, or a large-sized or odd-shaped piece, produces a focal point in a room that started out as a humble "box." These components are especially important in mid-century buildings, which are often devoid of detail and have less generous rooms and lower ceiling heights.

The design of doors between rooms also helps define the architectural look of a house. Classical architecture, historic periods, and European and other international influences can all inspire the design of interesting and unusual doors, which might have applied panels covered in leather or thick nailheads forming simple patterns. Doors can be rustic in a modern setting, or contemporary in a traditional home. They can be sophisticated or whimsical.

MUSIC
ZOLA
D-DAY
PARIS

HAMPTONS GARDENS

Classic paneling exhibits a twist by running the wood grain in two different directions, creating a two-tone effect.

A loft comes with intrinsic architectural detail. The original weight-bearing columns punctuate the space, as do the brick walls.

Fireplaces provide an opportunity to inject an architectural statement into a room, which creates atmosphere, and they, too, vary from highly traditional to ultramodern. I am passionate about fireplaces and was lucky enough to have one in my first graduate-school apartment. During a short period when I lived without one, I installed a mantel so that I could always feel as if there was one nearby. When I lived in a loft in SoHo, I installed two working fireplaces that I designed and created, one of plaster and one of wood. I later moved into a house that had seven. In winter I use the fireplace daily. I can hardly think of a more inspiring or relaxing treat.

The role of cabinetry is primarily functional, but it is an area in which architectural detail can be achieved despite budget. The height, materials, and decorative design of cabinetry contribute to the balance, symmetry, and scale of a room. Wooden cabinetry can be upholstered in leather, covered with grass cloth, or painted a different color or finish. Lighting can be incorporated to accentuate depth, structure, or detail, and mirrors, fabric, or paper inserts can be used to create a layered effect.

Architectural detailing is the cornerstone of this Hamptons living room. The fireplace wall is a series of set-back steps covered in stone, and the ceiling detail is created with a grid of applied moldings. Architectural elements such as the leather-woven sofa edging adds to the room's structured look.

Here, Dessins "created" architecture. The walls are clad in cerused leather by Edelman, and punctuated with strips of matching cerused wood.

Maker's Mark
GREY GOOSE
GREY GOOSE

Rooms and homes generally fall into one of two categories: standard-issue spaces with white walls and eight-foot-high ceilings versus spaces rich with architectural detail, be it traditional moldings and embellishments or modern sleek lines. Where a space is replete with architectural features I typically embrace them as the basis for the interior design. But with a tabula rasa, architectural detailing—whether classical and refined or contemporary and creative—should be considered to make the most of your space.

This crisp yet inviting kitchen combines strong architectural strokes with beachy materials. Blanc cassée cabinets combined with matte walnut by Christopher Peacock are structured but casual at once.

OPPOSITE This kitchen combines large-scale room dimensions with architectural detailed ceiling design.

ABOVE A smaller scale kitchen can still be enhanced architecturally, in this case with horizontal tile faux wood slats.

PABLO PICASSO: A RETROSPECTIVE
A Vanished World ROMAN VISHNIAC

One can be creative with bathroom vanities—each of these illustrates unique flair.

A plain rectangular white shell was entirely transformed by following the outlines of the pebble tiles as it travels around the room.

Architecture impacts design both inside and out. The strong architecture marries with strong bold dramatic furniture.

The architectural lines, reminiscent of Tuscan architecture, required strong statement furnishings to balance it. The Dedon hanging swing is dramatic and adds a focal point.

FURNITURE SHAPE AND STRUCTURE

“THE QUESTION OF WHAT YOU WANT TO OWN IS ACTUALLY THE QUESTION OF HOW YOU WANT TO LIVE YOUR LIFE.”

—Marie Kondo

There is such a vast array of furniture styles that it may seem a daunting subject to tackle. But setting style aside, the furniture plan is essential before starting to furnish a room. Furniture layouts are an art, and a clever use of space can make all the difference in the usability and attractiveness of a room.

Begin by defining how you will use a particular room. Who will use it: adults, children, family, or friends? What is the use of the room: relaxing, playing, entertaining, dining, or television? Does it need to be formal or informal, for guests or only for family? Next, make a list of the furniture required for the room to function. This will include standard pieces such as seating and tables and also any specialized furniture, for example a card table or desk. The placement of doors and windows should be taken into account, and the size of the space will influence the amount of furniture and the scale of the selected pieces. A room shouldn't look or feel overly cluttered or too spare.

Depending on the size of the room, a seating group typically consists of a sofa, two lounge chairs, a coffee table, and one or more end tables. Larger sofas anchor the cluster and can be placed against a wall or float in the middle of a room. A fireplace, television, piano, even the view can provide a focal point for the room. Place tall pieces, such as an étagère, cabinet, or wardrobe, where they visually balance the windows or doors. There are no hard and fast rules for furniture layouts—and don't be afraid to try imaginative arrangements. The beauty of furniture is that you can nearly always rearrange it.

CAPRI

Why settle for the expected, when every piece of furniture can be a work of art? I designed the half-round sofa clad in reclaimed timber, by Bespoke by Luigi, creating a conversation piece. The roundabout is a twist on a classic piece, bringing it into the twenty-first century. The settee by Philippe Hurel in Paris is as chic as it is comfortable.

CAPRI
CAPRI by the sea
Skira
ITALIAN GARDENS

There are many styles of furniture to choose from, but you will naturally be drawn to one style more than others, whether contemporary, traditional, or something in between. Shelter magazines and design and lifestyle websites offer a limitless source of inspirational imagery to help define which style or styles you prefer. When shopping look for furniture with staying power to create a timeless setting and maximize your investment. Furniture from the 1920s and early 1930s, when "modern" design first emerged, is still consistent with furniture design today, proving its longevity.

Consider how the pieces you like best will work together by evaluating their similarities and differences. Complementary forms create cohesive and harmonious settings. Unusual pieces add style, whimsy, and originality to a room—don't overlook them. Pair a simple sofa with a funky club chair, or choose more subdued club chairs if the sofa is the conversation piece.

OPPOSITE All upholstered club chairs are further embellished by using different fabric on the legs than on the body of the chair.
ABOVE A room is more interesting when combining both new and vintage pieces. Here, a bespoke Promemoria sofa edged in leather is married with a mid-century coffee table. With its sliding top, it's interesting filled with coffee-table books or a collection.

Today furnishings should be anything but standard-issue. The Lucite coffee table with its four ottomans, and the unusual twist on the game table are examples.

Mixing furniture from different eras creates a more personalized and individual room, but it can be perplexing to know what works together and what doesn't. Modern and contemporary pieces, for example, tend to mix well with those of the 1920s and 1930s from France as well as with mid-century modern. That doesn't mean you can't do a thoroughly contemporary look with an outrageous Louis piece. Antique and vintage furniture and accessories add a rich layer of interest, character, and refinement to a setting. It is merely a question of taste.

While most anything goes today, the desire for easy, relaxed living has driven the strong trend for more casual, modern décor and a rejection of all that's considered traditional. But anyone with knowledge of the late-twentieth century will know that ultramodern 1970s furniture gave way to the uber-traditional 1980s. No one would have believed that cool restraint would swing back with the new millennium.

The placement of a sofa at the base of a bed, facing a television, or fireplace, is a practical and luxurious way to dress a bedroom.

Furniture styles must be carefully considered in a room designed around an art collection.

When the furniture pieces are unique, it is important to balance the color scheme and patterns.

Interesting furniture requires thought to how it is combined—varying shapes and textures is important to create a balanced mix.

The indoor/outdoor grill and pizza oven are so dramatic, that the Sutherland dining table and chairs are a restrained, handsome accompaniment.

COLOR PALETTE AND POLISH

"COLOR DOES NOT ADD A PLEASANT QUALITY TO DESIGN—IT REINFORCES IT."

—Pierre Bonnard

The selection and use of color is one of the most complex subjects in interior decoration and design. To color, or not to color—that is the question. Color influences mood, and the color scheme of a room can have psychological and physiological effects.

Taste is constantly changing in the realm of color. Think of the dark, heavy colors used in Victorian times, the bland colors of the 1950s, the bright psychedelics characterizing the 1970s, and the overly colorful prints, papers, and fabrics of the 1980s and 1990s. Today the predominant color palettes are grays, blues, and whites, often with bright accents such as orange, turquoise, and vibrant blues. There are numerous variations of white, and each offers a serene, consistent look as well as a crisp background for any style of design. Gray, so popular today, is easy on the eye; it can be part of a monochromatic color scheme or provide a backdrop to a more varied color palette. In certain parts of the United States, such as the South, strong color is used more often and more liberally. In color-drenched rooms, the emphasis is usually on bright hues, for example red, orange, and blue, which are paired with neutrals, such as white, cream, and beige.

France
A HISTO

Most color is applied through painting, and the choice of paint is paramount to the overall look of a room. Besides the actual color, paint has other qualities that affect its decorative value. Different finishes, from high gloss on one end of the scale to matte on the other, with semi-gloss, eggshell, satin, and flat in between, have different connotations. Not just a gradation of shine, each finish has its own properties and is meant for different applications. Eggshell can be wiped down, but flat-finish paint cannot. There are paints that offer a sense of texture, or give the appearance of velvet, chalk, or limestone. Certain paint manufacturers distinguish themselves by means of these specialty paints.

Today almost museum-quality paint techniques are being employed. A lacquer finish can simulate back-painted glass, creating a mirror surface of color. It takes weeks to achieve, but the result can take your breath away. Other techniques contribute meaningfully to the aesthetic of a room. Venetian plaster was all the rage at the end of the twentieth century, and it became a catch-all expression for any shiny plaster paint finish. In reality it is much more.

The blue lacquered walls, done in the authentic traditional way marry with the same blue back-painted glass to create a "wow."

Neutrals are a perfect backdrop for bold blues.

BVLGARI
PATRICK DEMARCHELIER

Color is part of one's self expression in design and should be considered carefully in creating your overall design scheme. Paint can be a complementary backdrop in a design or an integral feature in the overall look. I am not a fan of the feature wall, which strikes me as contrived. If you select a non-neutral color, however, use it continuously, fully wrapping or enveloping a room. Or make a statement with the creative use of color, such as the ombré design illustrated here, where the draperies are in harmony with the painted walls.

Color makes this "bunk room" come alive.

One of everyone's favorite rooms, this library gets its dreamy look by combining true gray with strong lavender.

Great American Cook
SUPERCHEFS

DREAMHOUSE

The use of orange is repeated throughout the outdoor terraces and dining areas. Here it is cushions, but vases and end-tables dot the gardens.

FABRIC FIBER AND FLAIR

> TEXTILES ARE A COMMON THREAD IN ALL OUR LIVES. CORRESPONDING TO THE MANY GEARS WE ALL MOVE THROUGH IN THE COURSE OF OUR DAY-WORK, REFLECTION, REST, LEVITY AND LOVE—THEY SPEAK TO OUR SENSES ON AN EMOTIONAL LEVEL. THROUGH TEXTURE AND COLOR, THEY CAN INFLUENCE OUR MOODS, JOG OUR MEMORY, AND SIMPLY SPEAK TO WHO WE ARE—FUNCTIONING AS A FORM OF SELF-EXPRESSION.

—Lori Weitzner

The history of textiles dates back thousands of years. It is one of the common threads that weave together cultures and regions. While decorative textile work dates from more than a thousand years ago, archaeologists have discovered a fabric fragment from about 7000 BC and sewing needles that may be 50,000 years old!

There has always been a practical and functional relationship between textiles and décor. Fabric is used for insulation, warmth, and comfort: curtains block drafts and regulate internal temperatures, and upholstery makes it more comfortable for us to sit. Fabrics are made using a variety of fibers and techniques, giving us cottons, linens, velvets, sheers, flannels, taffetas, silks, and many more. While the basic weave may remain constant, colors, patterns, textures, and methods of use are subject to the same fashions and trends that have influenced the design of interiors throughout history.

Drapery lends warmth to a space, both literally and figuratively, makes a ceiling appear higher, camouflages a bad view, augments architectural dimension, and almost always adds lovely softness to a room. Draperies are steeped in tradition but can be the height of modernity. A simple header trimming a window is clean and uncomplicated. A sheer blind lets in natural light but still offers privacy, and a shade can block out light in a bedroom.

Upholstered walls are often dismissed today—wrongly, to my mind. They give value and dimension to a room that can often only be created with some other architectural embellishment such as moldings or woodwork. Whether walls are upholstered with flat linen, thick velvet, a wild or subtle pattern, or store-bought sheets (like I used in college), they create an environment. Upholstered walls transform plain white boxes into unique and personalized spaces.

Upholstered pieces and soft goods, such as throw pillows, are important components of a room. Today, the fabric scheme for a furniture ensemble often combines solid colors with texture to provide visual and tactile interest. Prints always have a place in interior design, despite the current trend for simplicity. And a room with cool prints and bold patterns can look sharply modern. The mantra "less is more" is alive and well today, so prints tend to be used sparingly; on the other hand, nothing prevents you from designing an entire room around a print.

Fabric can never be underestimated in room design. Today texture is the most important adjective.

Throw pillows pull a fabric scheme together. They can be big, especially when a sofa has no separate back cushions; or they can be smaller additions. There are also oblong, lumbar, and every oddly shaped cushion you can imagine. Pillows have different patterns and colors, and bold prints can be used to enliven a neutral scheme. I like to mix both sizes and patterns. If a sofa is very long, I might add a rectangular lumbar in the center. A larger pillow in a solid would be accompanied by a slightly smaller pillow with more color, texture, or pattern. Trim for each pillow would vary in size and color, while the back panel might consist of an interesting secondary fabric. I avoid repeating the same fabric over and over in the same room—I would never use a window fabric on a pillow or chair.

The use of trim has been pared back in recent times, but don't overlook it. Trim adds a layer of richness to a design. A plain, flat tape creates a fine, bespoke look. Cords and moss fringe, instead of bouillon and tassels, are suitable for finishing a modern setting. On throw pillows, trim can be leather piping, cord, or flat tape in any unusual pattern or color.

Fabric is one aspect of interior design in which practicalities must be taken into account. When choosing a textile, consider its suitability not only for day-to-day life but also the maintenance it requires. Fabrics are not as delicate as they once were: many contemporary indoor and outdoor fabrics have technical properties that improve their durability and keep them in good repair.

The cool lavender and gray palette is enhanced by geometric fabrics.

FLOORING CRAFT AND FINISH

"

ONE MAN'S CEILING IS ANOTHER MAN'S FLOOR.

"

—Paul Simon

Flooring unifies a room, provides a stage for furnishings, and also defines seating groups. And like everything else in interior design, flooring changes with tastes and trends. Wall-to-wall carpet was the epitome of modern design and a symbol of upward mobility in the mid-twentieth century. Today, there is a strong preference for area rugs that cover only part of the floor.

Carpet and area rugs are both valid choices, as is having no carpet at all. But if the floor is visible, the material must be selected to complement the style of the room. Floors can be pre-finished or stained wood, rustic or natural stone, sleek marble, or concrete. There are a large number of possibilities within each category.

Wood brings a sense of warmth to a space. It can be laid straight or on an angle; in a herringbone or chevron pattern; in wide or narrow planks; with a matte or shiny finish; and stained in any tone from a black matte to a white wash. Gray wood is a rather new and immensely coveted look. Stone is cooler and sleeker than wood and it can be laid as a slab or cut into tiles ranging from small mosaics to large sizes. Large rectangular tiles are very popular today.

Thick planks work well in beach environments.

Rugs are experiencing a renaissance, and the diversity of rug types is astonishing. Manufacturers have become ever more creative in producing rugs and carpeting that was unimaginable at the turn of the twenty-first century. Cowhide rugs have proliferated in recent years. Interesting patterns and colors have emerged, and cowhide always looks clean, even white cowhide. Rugs combining wool and silk have a luxurious texture; in some cases, synthetics substitute for silk to keep the price in check. Solid-colored rugs and carpets, often with thick borders, are increasingly popular. Stylish flat-weave rugs and carpets are versatile and easy to clean and can be used in many settings. Flat weaves made from natural fibers, such as cotton or wool, woven with a chevron pattern, stripes, or tweed are inviting in any room and particularly useful on stairs. Sisal has matured, and there are dozens of patterns and color tonalities available. They are woven with natural fibers as well as fabricated in jute/sisal combinations, synthetics, and wool. Sisal and its cousins add casual elegance to urban and country residences. Don't be afraid to use a simple sisal in the most elaborately designed room: it will ground the space and add a chic touch.

The octagonal Carrara marble is a counterfoil to the square tub and counter design.

The binding of a rug can be the simple end finish of a weave, or a border can be applied. Many wool rugs have a border woven in, but there are also numerous types of borders that can be added or sewn on, such as canvas, leather, or patterns.

Determining the size of an area rug is best done with a floor plan. Many carpet vendors will measure a room gratis, as they do for wall-to-wall carpet. An area rug is used to define or anchor a furniture setting, and its size should be determined by the placement of the pieces. It can sit within a seating arrangement or extend around it. There is no one-size-fits-all solution, but leave at least 18 inches between the wall and the edge of the rug. If budget allows, opt for a larger rug rather than a smaller one.

This skyroom is flooded with light and angular motifs. The velvet quilted fabric on the sofas repeat the tile motif.

LIGHTING LUSTER AND RADIANCE

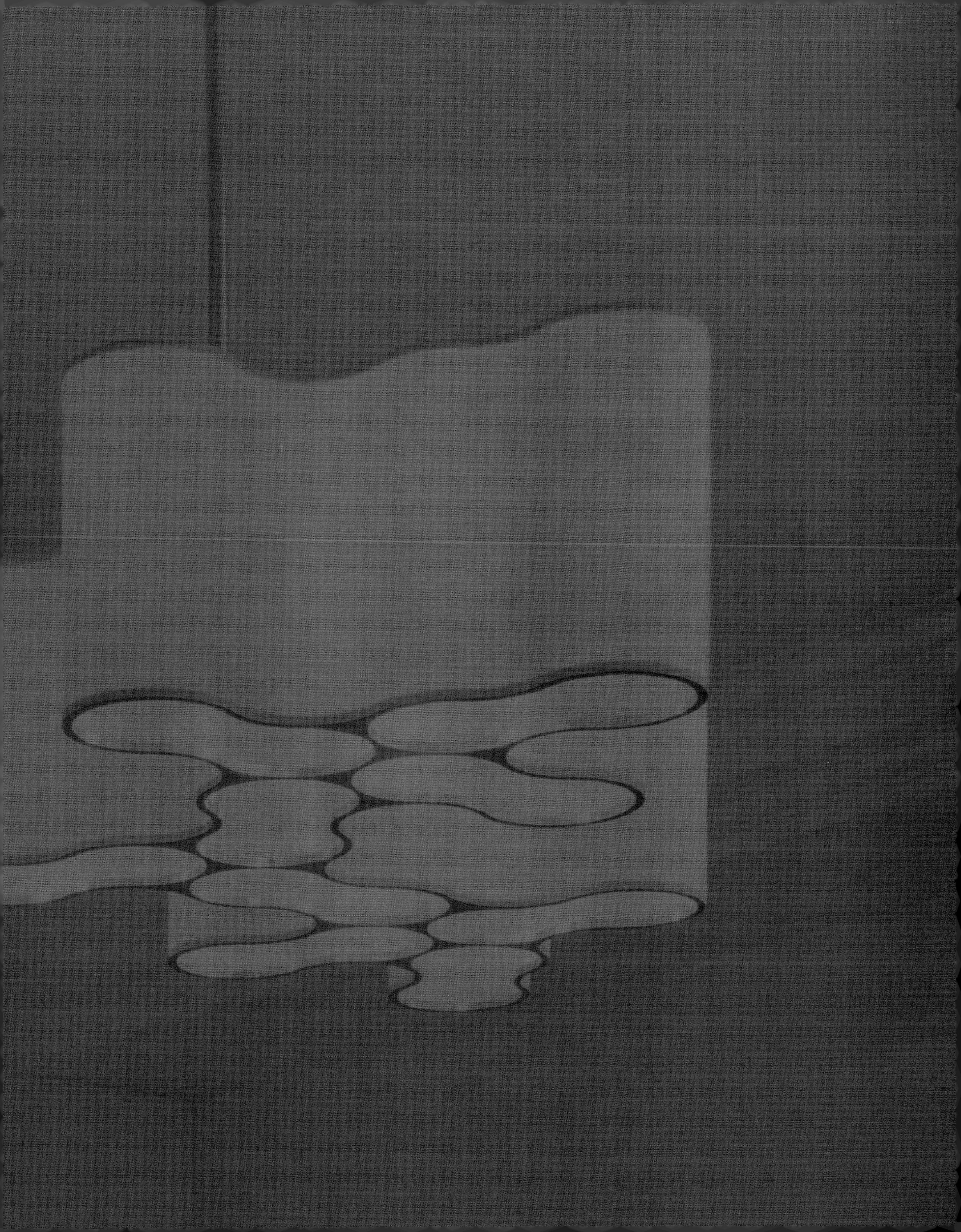

"

A ROOM IS LIKE A STAGE. IF YOU SEE IT WITHOUT LIGHTING, IT CAN BE THE COLDEST PLACE IN THE WORLD.

"

—Paul Lynde

Lighting placement is monumentally important in room design and function.

Lighting is just as reactive to design trends and innovations as any other element of an interior, and the effects of technological advances are evident throughout the twentieth century—can you imagine the 1970s without track lighting? Lighting plays a functional role in a room and at the same time contributes to its ambience or atmosphere. There is enormous variation in type and style of lighting fixtures—traditional chandeliers, contemporary pendants, subtle sconces, and small or large table and standing lamps with shades and light columns, and so on—and thus they make an important decorative contribution to a space.

A lighting plan starts with the furniture layout of a room and should include "layers of light," that is, light from different sources and angles. The number of lighting fixtures in a room is related to the size of that room, but it is better to err on the side of too many. Higher ceilings can obviously take larger fixtures, and can be supplemented with recessed lighting that can illuminate hard-to-reach corners.

Lighting is not just practical. It can be whimsical and, above all, beautiful.

Mid-century lighting, used judiciously, can make a strong statement.

I strongly recommend ceiling-mounted lights as opposed to recessed lights whenever possible. These can be single pendants, surface-mounted lights, multi-armed chandeliers, or groupings of pendants. Certain conditions, such as an apartment, may restrict your ability to install overhead lighting.

Less is definitely more when it comes to recessed lights. Once big and clunky, they are now available in small and stylish designs with different shapes and bezels that serve different functions and accommodate different types of bulbs, such as LEDs. Recessed fixtures can be placed in a grid or around the perimeter of a room to highlight walls and furniture.

Table and standing lamps add ambient light, which is an important factor in creating mood. Lamps can be any size and style, from serious to whimsical. Any of these can be wired for double bulbs, a modification that allows for more light. For table and standing lamps, don't forget to take the placement of electrical outlets into consideration. Floor outlets in particular help conceal wiring for lamps positioned in the middle of a room.

Sconces are especially useful in the absence of ceiling lights; moreover, they add to a room architecturally. They define the boundaries of an area and accentuate its features depending on placement. Wiring for sconces can be channeled up walls from the baseboard, and dimmers allow the level of lighting to be adjusted according to needs.

The right choice of lighting can seriously enhance the interior design scheme.

ABOVE These fantastic lights by Jonathan Wigmore are an artwork unto themselves.

Loving You More.

I especially like accessory lighting, such as bookcase lights and sconces, positioned above or on a bookcase. Pin spots applied to headboards, much like those mounted over business-class airline seats, are a practical choice for reading without disturbing your partner. Stair lights are meant to be functional but actually add such a soft, attractive glow that this may be a case of form over function. There are a slew of mid-century table lamps that have sculptural presence, and furniture and lighting designers have revived this concept with table lamps—luminescent shapes that are a good-looking addition to a buffet or console.

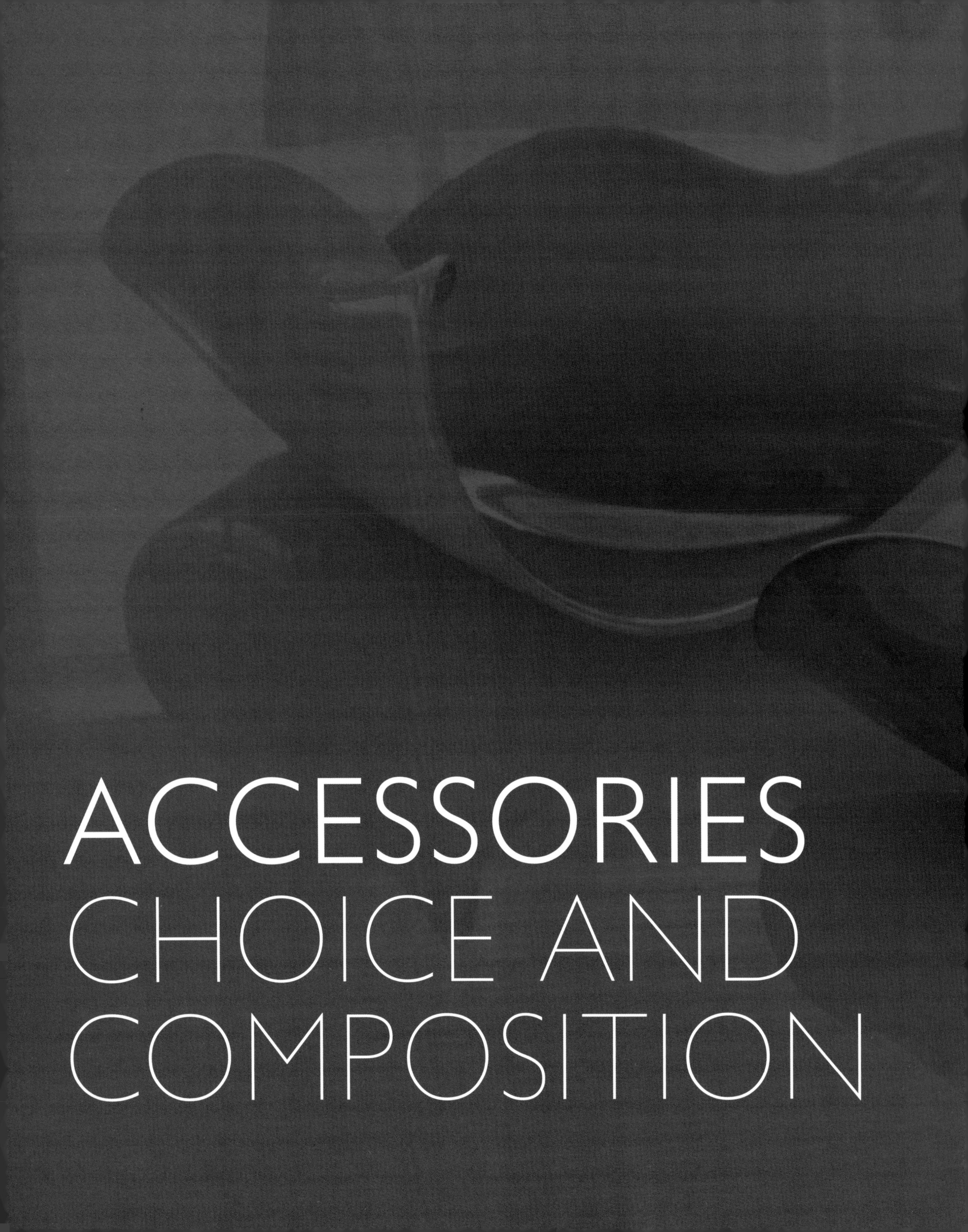

ACCESSORIES CHOICE AND COMPOSITION

“PEOPLE'S LIVES ARE EXPRESSED IN LITTLE DETAILS.”

—CHARLOTTE MOSS

Accessories complete a room. All the wonderful architectural features, furnishings, lighting, and more can produce a space that seems cold or uninviting—like a model room or hotel—without the many accoutrements that enrich and finish the design. Accessories include art, photographs, boxes, bowls, candlesticks, fireplace accessories, trays, throw pillows, sculptures, books, vases, flower, mirrors, and so on. The list is almost endless.

The best way to begin accessorizing is to evaluate what you already own, such as family photos, meaningful heirlooms, and decorative objects or artworks. Allocate them logically: books are generally housed in a bookcase, but why not try a coffee table or a stack next to the sofa? Candlesticks can be placed on a dining or end table; vases on a buffet or entrance table. Fill the larger spaces and work down to smaller areas and niches.

Groupings of objects, whether similar or different, can create interesting vignettes and arrangements. Place a ceramic or glass bowl on top of a small stack of coffee-table books; include good-sized candlesticks alongside. The idea is to vary the heights, sizes, and textures to balance the setting and the piece of furniture they are placed on. Bookcases are an ideal place to exhibit framed photos of family and friends. Assemble groups of frames with different heights and orientations, such as a tall vertical and a medium horizontal. Large frames can look good at each end of a row of books. There are no hard and fast rules—just enjoy collecting and displaying. Over time you can edit your collections. I personally prefer to use bookcases just for books and, as in many areas of design, remember that less is more.

The right accessories complement the furnishings and architecture. The étagère console (opposite) from the Marché aux Puces Paris is enhanced by the vintage mirror from Bernd Goeckler and the small accessories collected from a variety of places.

Throw pillows are not only comfortable but essential in completing a seating area. The "Penny Ottoman" was designed in 1985.

Art makes this beautiful entrance edgy.

Clothes may make the man (and woman!), but accessories make the home. This Dallas homeowner has been collecting these pieces with me for more than 25 years.

VAN GOGH IN ARLES
Degas Landscapes
KAUFMANN
FALLINGWATER
ABBEVILLE

Fireplaces need dressing up. Besides utilitarian items, such as andirons, fire screens, and tools, the mantel, with the right accessories, can become a compelling focal point. Because fireplaces are often surmounted by a mirror, artwork, or television, objects should be respectfully sized so that they do not block or distract from what is above.

Televisions have become decorative features in the twenty-first century. Once relegated to closets and armoires, they are now accepted parts of an interior design scheme due to their streamlined hi-tech looks. Spaces are designed with the presence of a television as a given rather than a necessary evil.

Hardware cannot be underestimated in importance. A penchant for polished nickel, common in the early 2000s, has shifted toward bronze. Many other finishes, such as metal with faux leather or fabric inserts, real-leather handles, and hardware made from blown glass, are all distinctive choices for doors, drawers, and cabinets. In some cases, an oversized handle makes a statement; in others, a modest finger grip provides a discreet, clean choice.

Bringing Paris Home
THE NEW FRENCH INTERIOR
Brasseries de Paris

NEW YORK 1900
THE TRAVIS INVITATIONAL

Art and sculpture are personal expressions of who we are.

ABOVE This new age étagère is filled with the client's collections.
OPPOSITE This entrance illustrates that less can be more—the two stunning vases are all that's needed.

YVES SAINT LAURENT
MODERN WOMEN
Sol LeWitt
BURRI

Accessories should express our life experiences. Add them over time, picking them up on vacation or at a flea market or vintage store. Yet there are so many interesting objects available in stores and online that there is great appeal in finessing the look of a room straightaway.

Either way, accessories are not optional extravagances. They are the spices that make the dish, the icing that makes the cake, the absolutely essential elements that make or break the overall look. Accessories equal personality.

"DESIGN IS AN OPPORTUNITY TO CONTINUE TELLING THE STORY, NOT JUST TO SUM EVERYTHING UP."

—TATE LINDEN

SOURCES

1st Dibs
200 Lexington Avenue
New York, New York 10016

Argosy Bookstore
116 East 59th Street
New York, New York 10022

Barney's
660 Madison Avenue
New York, New York 10065

Bergdorf Goodman
754 Fifth Avenue
New York, New York 10019

Bernd Goeckler Antiques
30 East 10th Street
New York, New York 10003

BK Antiques
306 East 61st Street
New York, New York 10065

Bruno Moinard Editions
31 rue Jacob
Paris 75006
France

Carlos de la Puente
209 E. 59th Street
New York, New York 10022

Casa di Bianco
866 Lexington Avenue
New York, New York 10065

Craig Van de Brulle
129 Elizabeth Street
New York, New York 10016

David Duncan
247 East 60th Street
New York, New York 10022

Delisle
4 rue Parc Royal
Paris 75003
France

End of History
548 ½ Hudson Street #A
New York, New York 10014

English Country Antiques
26 Snake Hollow Road
Bridgehampton, New York 11932

Eric Appel
306 East 61st Street
New York, New York 10022

Espaces 54
54 rue Mazarine
Paris 75006
France

Flair
88 Grand Street
New York, New York 10013

Flair
Lungarno Corsini 24r
Florence 50123
Italy

Frette
799 Madison Avenue
New York, New York

Galerie l'Arc en Seine
31 rue de Seine
Paris 75006
France

Galerie Andre Hayat
23 Rue de Lille
Paris 75007
France

Galerie Herve Van der Straeten
11 rue Ferdinand Duval
Paris 75004
France

Galeries des Lampes
9 rue de Beaune
Paris 75007
France

Galerie Jean-Louis Deniot
58 rue de l'Universite
Paris 75007
France

Galerie Makassar-France
19 avenue Matignon
Paris 75008
France

Galerie Pouenat
13 passage Dauphine
Paris 75006
France

Galerie Sylvain Levy-Alban
14 rue de Beaune
Paris 75007
France

Hermès
17 rue de Seine
Paris 75006
France

High Style Deco
224 West 18th Street
New York, New York 10011

Holland & Sherry
979 Third Avenue
New York, New York 10022

Jean de Merry
973 Third Avenue
New York, New York 10022

Jean Perzel
3 rue de la Cité Universitaire
Paris 75014
France

John Roselli
306 East 61st Street
New York, New York 10022

John Salibello
229 East 60th Street
New York, New York 10022

L'Art de Vivre
978 Lexington Avenue
New York, New York 10021

Le Douze
12 rue Jacob
Paris 75006
France

Maison Gerard
53 East 10th Street
New York, New York 10003

Mantiques Modern
146 West 22nd Street
New York, New York 10011

Mecox
962 Lexington Avenue
New York, New York 10021

Philippe Hurel
4 Ter Rue du Bouloi
Paris 75001
France

Promemoria
Via Bagutta, 13 /
Via Montenapoleone 8
Milan 20121
Italy

Ralph Pucci
44 West 18th Street
New York, New York 10011

Rizzoli Bookstore
1133 Broadway
New York, New York 10010

Silver Peacock
306 East 61th Street
New York, New York 10022

Venfield
227 East 60th Street
New York, New York 10022

ACKNOWLEDGMENTS

To my Interior Design support system,

Jorge Arango
Lisa Dewart Bingham
Michael Boodro
Mario Buatta
Charles Cohen
Lisa and James Cohen
Kendell Constrom
CJ Dellatore
Jamie Drake
Alicia Forzano
Luigi Gentile
Elizabeth Gill
Cary and Lisa Kravet
Walter and Lisa Kunzel
Mark Luedeman
Maggie Mardre
Andrea Monfried
Isabelle O'Connell
Krissa Rossbund
Mark Sacco
Elizabeth Sechrest
Steven and John Stark
Jacqueline Terrebonne
Newell Turner
Irwin Weiner
Lori Weitzner
Benny Zale

and Family and Friends,

Freddy, Adam, Alex, Benjamin, Philip, Jamie, Arie, Tina, Ashlie, Crystal

Barbara, Gail, Nina, Emma, Linda, Gilda, Stella, Dana, Jennifer, Vanessa,
Christel, Bonnie, Andrea, Cydonia, Gael, Laura

Nina & Andrew, Jason & Julie, Vicki & Sam, Laura & Daniel,
Joe, Sheila & David, Michelle & Michael, Lisa, Anna & Alex, Keren & Mark,
Marc & Randi, Kathy & Richard

And a special thanks to the talented Andrea Monfried, Nicole Boehringer,
Paul Latham, and all my friends at IMAGES